THE METER

AN EARLY METRIC BOOK

THE METER

by WILLIAM J. SHIMEK

pictures by George Overlie

Lerner Publications Company • Minneapolis

In the Early Metric books, we have used the "er" spellings of "meter" and "liter" in order that young readers may easily recognize and pronounce these words. The "re" spellings of the metric measurements—"metre," "litre," "kilometre"—are, of course, also correct and are commonly used in other countries. Reports issued by the U. S. Office of Education indicate the possibility that the United States will eventually adopt the "re" forms of these words.

LIBRARY OF CONGRESS CATALOGING IN PUBLICATION DATA

Shimek, William J.
    The meter.

    (An Early Metric Book)
    SUMMARY: Describes the way length, distance, width, and height are measured in meters.

    1. Metric system—Juvenile literature. [1. Metric system] I. Overlie, George, ill. II. Title.

QC92.5.S476 1975   389'.152   74-11894
ISBN 0-8225-0586-X

Published simultaneously in Canada by J. M. Dent & Sons (Canada) Ltd., Don Mills, Ontario.

Manufactured in the United States of America.

International Standard Book Number: 0-8225-0586-X
Library of Congress Catalog Card Number: 74-11894

Second Printing 1976

389.152   c7
   Sh   # 8

1. Metric system

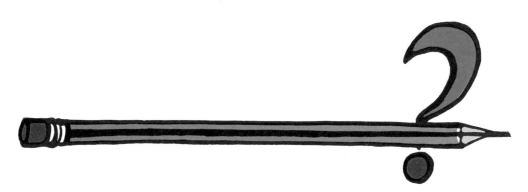

How long is a pencil?

How thick is a slice of bread?

How tall is a horse?

How wide is this board?

How far is it to the store?

What is the length of this bug?

To measure how long or how far . . .

use the METER.

To measure how thick

or how tall

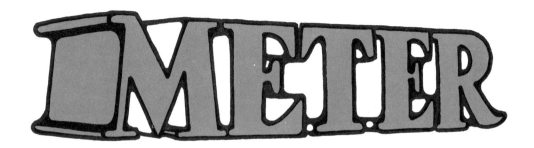

or how wide . . .

use the METER.

Small lengths are often measured with the . . .

MILLImeter.

Width of a pencil—
about 7 millimeters

Width of a pencil lead—
about 2 millimeters

Thickness of heavy posterboard—
about 1 millimeter

Length of a mosquito—
about 6 millimeters

Here are some lengths that can be measured with
the millimeter.

Small lengths can also be measured with the . . .

CENTImeter.

Here are some lengths that can be measured with
the centimeter.

Length of a housefly —
about 1 centimeter

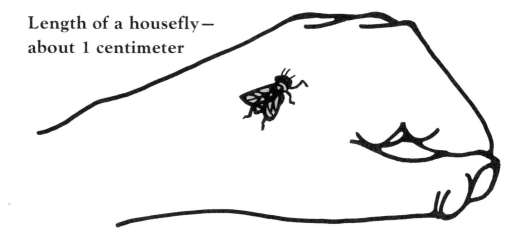

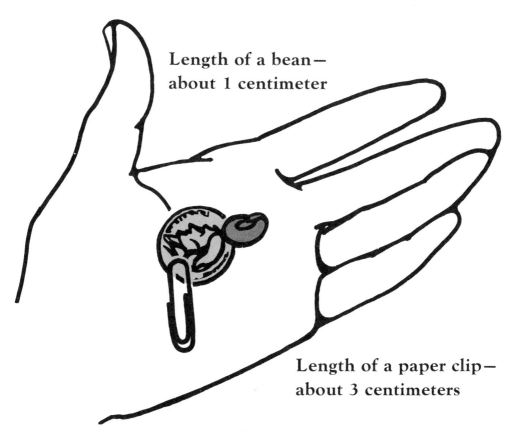

Length of a bean—
about 1 centimeter

Length of a paper clip—
about 3 centimeters

Diameter of a nickel—about 2 centimeters

Diameter of a nickel—
20 millimeters

A CENTIMETER

has the same length as

10

MILLIMETERS.

Diameter of a nickel—
2 centimeters

Many lengths can be measured with either

the CENTIMETER

or

the MILLIMETER.

Length of a housefly—
1 centimeter

Length of a housefly—
10 millimeters

Here are some lengths that can be measured with the decimeter.

A DECIMETER

has the same length as

10

CENTIMETERS.

Diameter of a nickel—2 centimeters

10 CENTIMETERS = 1 DECIMETER

A DECIMETER

has the same length as

100

MILLIMETERS.

Diameter of a nickel — 20 millimeters

100 MILLIMETERS = 1 DECIMETER

Many lengths can be measured with either

DECIMETERS

or

CENTIMETERS

or

MILLIMETERS.

Length of a piece of chalk —
1 decimeter or 10 centimeters
or 100 millimeters

Width of a sheet of notebook paper—
2 decimeters or 20 centimeters
or 200 millimeters

Length of a pencil—
2 decimeters or
20 centimeters or
200 millimeters

Pretend that you have a stick that is
exactly 1000 millimeters long.

The length of this stick has
a very special name.

It is called a
METER.

Every meter has the same length as

1000 MILLIMETERS

or

100 CENTIMETERS

or

10 DECIMETERS.

Ask your parents or your teacher to show you a meter stick.

Look at it.

Hold it in your hand.

Many lengths can be measured with the meter.

A large dog is about 1 meter long.

You are probably just a little taller than 1 meter.

A bicycle is about 1 meter high.

Your classroom is about 10 meters long.

Ten meters is called a DEKAmeter.

Your classroom is about 1 dekameter long.

A football field is about 100 meters long.

One hundred meters is called a HECTOmeter.

A football field is about 1 hectometer long.

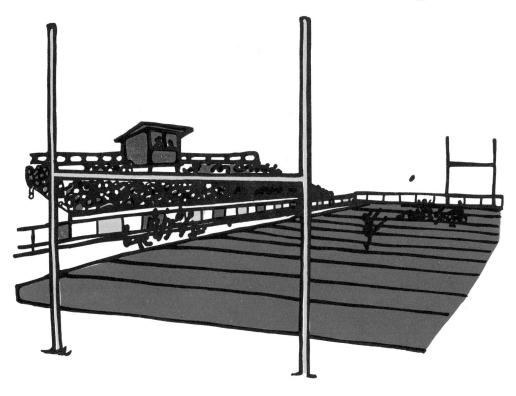

Someday you may run 1000 meters in a race.

One thousand meters is called a KILOmeter.

So you would run 1 kilometer.

The distance from New York City to Chicago

is about

1300 kilometers.

The distance from the earth to the moon
is about
375,000 kilometers.

It is about 150,000,000 kilometers
from the earth to the sun.

The name of each of the measures in this book has a shorter form.

KILOMETER ▶ KM

HECTOMETER ▶ HM

DEKAMETER ▶ DAM

METER ▶ M

DECIMETER ▶ DM

CENTIMETER ▶ CM

MILLIMETER ▶ MM

MARTIN

10 MILLIMETERS (MM) = 1 CENTIMETER (CM)
100 MILLIMETERS (MM) = 1 DECIMETER (DM)
1000 MILLIMETERS (MM) = 1 METER (M)

10 CENTIMETERS (CM) = 1 DECIMETER (DM)
100 CENTIMETERS (CM) = 1 METER (M)

10 DECIMETERS (DM) = 1 METER (M)

10 METERS (M) = 1 DEKAMETER (DAM)
100 METERS (M) = 1 HECTOMETER (HM)
1000 METERS (M) = 1 KILOMETER (KM)

10 DEKAMETERS (DAM) = 1 HECTOMETER (HM)
100 DEKAMETERS (DAM) = 1 KILOMETER (KM)

10 HECTOMETERS (HM) = 1 KILOMETER (KM)

ABOUT THE AUTHOR

William J. Shimek has taught mathematics for many years in the public schools of Minnesota. He has made good use of his extensive classroom experience as well as his knowledge of mathematics in writing this series of metric books for young readers. A native of Minnesota, Mr. Shimek received a master's degree in math education from Florida State University in 1972. Since 1961, he has taught mathematics at Brooklyn Center Junior-Senior High School in Brooklyn Center, Minnesota. In addition to his activities in professional organizations such as the National Council of Teachers of Mathematics, Mr. Shimek devotes his spare time to an unusual hobby — distance running — and to long bicycle trips with his family. He has also found time to write a math book for young readers entitled PATTERNS: WHAT ARE THEY? Mr. Shimek lives in Blaine, Minnesota, with his wife and four children.